# Connecting with Heaven:

## How to Be a
## Psychic Medium

# Rev. Martina Schmidt

Published by: Rev. Martina Schmidt LLC &
Joyful Living Publishing 2007
Distributed in the United States by www.lulu.com
Editorial Consultation: Kathleen Woodward

www.MartinaSchmidt.com
Joyful Living Center
2329 Silvernail Rd.
Pewaukee, WI 53072
(262) 522-8170
martina@martinaschmidt.com

**Second Edition-2008**
**ISBN#978-0-6151-9833-0**

*Acknowledgments*

Thank you to Todd for picking up the slack (and never complaining) so I could follow my dream,

…To Logan and Taylor for reminding me to believe in magic and the beauty of life,

…To my Mom for all her time, love and patience, especially with proof reading,

And

…To Joy for being the match that lit the fuse for a new life.

# *Contents*

# Introduction

## How I Became a Medium

*"Far away there in the sunshine are my highest aspirations.
I may not reach them, but I can look up and see their
beauty, believe in them, and try to follow where they lead."
--Louisa May Alcott*

Even as a small child my heart yearned for a God that I could trust. I wanted to believe my Sunday school teachers were wrong about God being something to fear. As I grew older questions would enter my mind during church. How could I love a God who would banish someone to hell because they felt deep loneliness and sadness and took their own life? How could I love a God who found pleasure in tossing souls into a lake of fire because they simply had doubt he existed? The answer was, I could not. And so, my dissatisfaction with God stayed with me for many years until the answers began to change.

"Embraced by the Light" by Betty J. Eadie was a book that came out in the early 90's, a time in my life filled with diapers and books on parenting. It was a sleepy, cold Wisconsin afternoon that my life took a turn. I had just sat down to feed my newborn son and to try to coax him into a nap. Oprah was on the television and Betty Eadie was the guest on the show. I had never heard of this simple, quiet woman, but watched mesmerized as she introduced me to a new phenomenon called the near death experience.

I felt great peace as she described her experience of dying unexpectedly in the hospital after a simple operation only to enter a most loving and magical place. She talked of passing through a long white tunnel of light and seeing her loved ones who had died waiting for her with open arms and smiles at the other end. She described beautiful gardens and the experience of feeling completely loved and at peace.

As she spoke, I felt tears growing inside of me, tears of remembering. Somewhere in my heart I yearned for what she was saying. I knew without a doubt she was speaking the truth and decided to buy her book.

That one book opened my world to a new truth- Heaven was real and Hell was not. God really did love every one of us. Love was the only reality after death! In remembering this truth, I made a decision to tell everyone I could about it. I had no idea the way I would bring this teaching through me. God, however, had very big plan!

As I changed my mind, my life began to change as well. At this time in my life, I was working as a nurse in a bone marrow transplant unit. Unfortunately, in this area of nursing the patients had a high probability of dying. Bone marrow transplant was usually a last ditch effort and many patients couldn't handle the strain on their bodies. As I look back now, it was the perfect place for me to begin learning about death.

I saw death for the first time in this unit and was shocked at how simplistic it was. The death I witnessed was a patient I had just met and so I wasn't emotionally involved in the whole experience. The patient was aware that she was dying and had a "no resuscitation" order, which meant she wouldn't have any measures taken to spare her life.

On the evening she died, I watched as her family surrounded her and said their goodbyes. She was in a deep sleep and it wasn't long before she took her last breath. It felt surreal as I watched the experience around me. I kept looking around expecting something, anything, to occur to indicate she was leaving us. Nothing came but silence and stillness.

I also had my first encounter with a deceased spirit while working for this unit, a young woman I'll call Anya. Anya was a beautiful patient in her early twenties who had leukemia. Every shift I worked, I spent time talking with her about the book I was reading on Heaven. She always seemed a little uncomfortable with the topic but couldn't resist asking me more questions when I would come into her room.

Anya had an 18-month-old son at home and she was fighting hard to stay alive for him. I wanted to help her in anyway I could. Because of her youth and desire for life, I couldn't imagine her losing the fight. Even so, she passed quickly and unexpectedly in the middle of the night when I was home with my family.

I was deeply saddened when I heard about her death. I cried myself to sleep that night. My own son was only two and I couldn't imagine leaving him behind without a mother. On top of that, it was the first time I had known anyone who was younger than me to die. I began to realize the preciousness of time and that life had no guarantees. Her death touched and changed my life.

A few days after her death I had an experience that changed my life and my career. I was sitting on the couch very relaxed watching my two children sleeping deeply next to me. I was contemplating a nap myself when I heard my name called out. It was the oddest sensation to hear my name called out when I was alone. My brain was quite confused and I blew it off as my imagination.

I closed my eyes, reconsidering that nap, when immediately an image popped into my mind of Anya. I could see her so clearly! She looked so different from the last time I had seen her. Her hair had grown back long, black and curly.

She was smiling and wearing a beautiful white dress. I heard her say, "Hello Martina. How are you?" Only, the words I heard came from inside of my mind not from the room around me.

I thought to myself, "Wow, what an imagination I have!" I wasn't even thinking of Anya and there she was in my head smiling and talking to me.

I began to ponder the idea that maybe this was real and a beautiful feeling pervaded my body. I knew she was at peace and was definitely not dead. She began to thank me for all the times we had spoken and to tell me the things I had shared with her about Heaven were accurate.

She explained to me she had been with her son and husband from the moment of her passing. She told me her son was totally aware of her presence and that he had smiled when he saw her. She told me everything was going to be ok and that she understood now why she couldn't stay. And then she was gone.

I never spoke about the experience with anyone. It was hard enough for me to believe, let alone inviting the doubts of my family and friends. So, I moved on thinking it was a one-time thing. Boy was I wrong!

Within the next few months I began to see lights around my patients and hear voices in my head telling me information about the patient. I would always ask the patient questions to verify the information I was receiving and it was almost always accurate! They would stare at me in disbelief and curiosity.

I must admit I was curious myself as to what was happening to me. I knew I either had a rare brain tumor causing hallucinations or these experiences were real and my reality was changing. Of course, it turned out to be the latter of the two.

As I allowed myself to accept what I was seeing as having value and meaning, my experiences began to increase. I was in a new nursing unit one evening doing pool nursing for a staffing agency. I noticed a mustard yellow energy around one of the other nurse's kidney area. It wasn't a pretty yellow, but muddied looking. Curious about what I was seeing, I blurted out, "Do you have problems with your kidneys?" The nurse, not knowing me at all, turned pale and walked away. I was embarrassed by her reaction and my impulsive behavior.

A few minutes later however, she came back and with tear filled eyes said, "How do you know about my kidneys?" She proceeded to tell me how she had struggled with kidney stones for many years now and was feeling hopeless about her situation as no doctor was able to help her. It was at that moment that I decided to explore how seeing these colors could teach me how to help other people.

I discovered a school that specialized in healing the human energy field, also called the aura. As I was taking this training I was required to practice what I learned with others.

It was during this practicing that I became aware that I could speak to those who had died.

From the very beginning, every person I practiced on had a spirit show up in the room that wanted to tell me something! At first, I had no idea what was going on. I though it was my imagination. But as I became braver and spoke out about what I was experiencing things changed.

Most of my clients were strangers to me and had been referred by their friends. So, it took an amazing amount of courage to tell them I was sensing a spirit in the room. I was very concerned, at this point in my life, with what people thought. Becoming an energy healer was already 'far out' so talking to the other side was a little 'farther out' than I was ready to go. However, I took the leap, opened my mouth and heart and life has never been the same.

When I began talking to spirits and realized I was a medium, I looked for help anywhere I could find it. Help was nowhere to be found. No one knew how to teach me what it was like to be a medium. In fact, most people thought I was crazy to even think I was one!

Now, 10 years later, I'm an international medium and help people from all over the world to talk to Heaven. I am a self-taught medium and have trained people to do exactly what I do. Yes, it is a process that can be learned by anyone! With a little patience and practice you can develop your abilities to talk to your loved ones on the other side and also the loved ones of everyone else. Are you ready to begin?

# Chapter 1

## What and where is Heaven?

*"The Kingdom of God does not come with your careful observation, nor will people say, 'Here it is,' or 'There it is,' because the Kingdom of God is within You." Luke17: 20-21*

In response to this question, I am sure most would repeat what they were told as a child. Because we have no way to truly know heaven without first dying, none of us can be an expert on the topic. However, we can look at scriptures which reference heaven and, if we are so inclined to believe in near death experiences, can research the idea of heaven by reading the experiences of those who claim to have been there and returned.

There are many books available on the topic and I suggest you research and read as many as you can. For the purpose of this book, I will only give my firsthand experiences from the communications I have had with those who exist there.

My understanding is still growing and changing. In the last ten years as a medium I have discovered these facts about Heaven.

- Heaven is a "State of Being" that we all return to when we let go of our physical body: an experience of oneness with everything and everyone.

- No one is denied the experience of Heaven unless they want to be denied and even this denying isn't permanent.

- Heaven is Infinite and Eternal- it has always been and always will be.

- Heaven is a frequency of vibration which is pure Love and that frequency is within everything that exists and can be "tuned into" anytime.

- Heaven is a finer vibration, a higher frequency of energy that occupies the space within us and around us.

- Heaven can be perceived in the physical body but not in its entirety.

- Animals are welcomed into Heaven and can communicate just as easily as people.

- Souls who weren't born but began growing in their mothers are alive and well.

- All in Heaven know each other. (This was quite a hard thing for my mind to grasp but, nonetheless, it is what I have been told by those on the other side.)

- Souls who have died can easily perceive the physical reality we are in, and often they enjoy being around us participating in our lives. They love to communicate with us and let us know they still exist.

- We continue to possess our personalities when we are in Heaven with the refinement of greater understanding & compassion.

- When we cross-over we experience the beauty and the pain that we brought to the world through the eyes of everyone we ever encountered.

- When we pass we go through a review of the life we lived and experience what it was like to be loved or harmed by us. We experience the cause and effect of all of our actions.

- It is perfectly OK for souls to communicate with those who are still in physical reality. Although they cannot give us information that may interfere with our own life choices, they are happy to encourage us to choose joy, love and forgiveness.

- Those that greet you when you cross have nothing to do with any particular religion! You will see who you expect to see- Jesus, Buddha, your loved ones etc. In Heaven they understand God has many faces but there's only One Creator.

In order to understand life continuing on to another reality after the physical body dies, we must first understand ourselves as more than our bodies. Quantum physics has had remarkable breakthroughs in the last decades proving we are more than physical matter. We are moving, thinking, and feeling vibrators!

Ok, I know you weren't expecting me to call you a vibrator but it's true, you are. You are particles of light vibrating at different frequencies, some of which are visible to your eye and most of which are not. In other words you are energy!

When we leave the physical reality, we simply leave behind the part of us that is visible to the physical eye. We become spiritual beings once again, like before we were born. Our memories, about being with God and the heavenly environment, are returned to us.

We are still able to perceive and participate somewhat on the physical level of reality, but our main focus is back onto the spiritual life. Joy, love and well-being are the feelings of heaven.

When we die, there are no illusions anymore about being separate from God or from anything at all! This gives the awareness that everything is in perfect order and so grief, anger and disappointment is released.

Many times people ask me why we don't get to keep memories of where we came from when we become physical beings. Well, to simply put it, it's because it would hurt way too much! We would be homesick all the time and would never enjoy our physical experience.

I have encountered quite a few clients who are already in this predicament and it is very difficult for them to appreciate anything in their lives. They are always thinking about dying and wanting to "go home". I am sure you have known someone like this. They miss all the fun of living and it is supposed to be fun. So, it's truly best for us if we come in fresh with our focus on the experience of living immersed in the illusion of separateness (that topic is another book altogether).

So, where is this Heaven? I cannot give you a physical location because the reality is when you are one with everything, as you are in Heaven, you are everywhere. So, in truth, heaven is everywhere! It is all around you externally and in every space within you. If you're mind is saying "huh?" you wouldn't be alone in your confusion. Suffice it to say, it's hard to grasp.

What's important is that you realize Heaven is reachable because it's inside you and all around you. The reason you don't see it physically is because Heaven vibrates at a frequency too fast for the human eye to perceive. But, there are ways to experience Heaven when you understand that it exists as vibration and you learn to pick up those vibrations and interpret them clearly.

# Chapter 2

## The Buzz on Energy
### *"And what is a man without energy?*
### *Nothing - nothing at all."*
### *Mark Twain*

Everything you see, touch, taste, smell, feel and think is energy. Energy cannot be created or be destroyed, it can only change form, such as when ice melts into water and then evaporates into a gas in the air. So, simply recognizing that we are beings made up of particles of energy, we know scientifically that we cannot be destroyed- death does not exist.

Everything is Energy. Einstein's 1905 formula $E = mc2$ explains the relationship between Energy and matter, i.e., that Energy and matter are interchangeable that, in reality, everything is Energy.

Quantum Physics has discovered a field of energy that is the root cause of all matter. Scientists are calling it "The Unified Field" or the "Zero-Point Field". All matter when broken down to the tiniest particles, turns into pure energy. This energy is everywhere at once and is not confined by time or space. Everything originates from and is connected to this field of energy. We are all one!

In the book "The Field", journalist Lynne McTaggart writes about scientists at respected universities who are researching the outer limits of what is considered scientifically acceptable. More or less by accident they seem to have discovered an ocean of vibrations, which seems to connect everything with everything else in the universe the Unified Field, a sort of invisible network.

Modern science has proven that all that we call matter and energy is but "modes of vibratory motion". Everything is in constant movement and vibration, but the differences between the various forms of matter are due entirely to the varying rate and mode of vibrations. Spirit is at one end of the pole of vibration, the other end being forms of matter. Between these two are millions upon millions of different rates and modes of vibration.

When we die our vibrations change from that of matter to the vibrations of spirit. Spirit's vibrations are so fast that it's difficult to see them with our physical eyes. We can however feel the vibrations of spirit. As we learn to recognize what spirit feels like, we can fine-tune this skill to identify what spirit is trying to tell us.

Because everything is energy, thoughts and feelings are also energy. Have you ever thought of someone and called him or her only to hear them say, "I was just thinking about you"? Your thoughts about them got to them before you could dial the phone! Thought energy travels faster than light.

It is instantaneous and can be picked up by anyone who wants to tune into it.

Have you ever walked into a room where an argument had just occurred and it felt stuffy or uncomfortable to you? You perceived the energy of those feelings in your energy field.

Feelings are vibrations that can also be tuned into. Let's say a friend near you feels love and appreciation for you. This creates and emits a vibration. You may tune into it and a feeling of warm fuzzies will come over you. They didn't have to say a word!

As a mother, I always know when my children are sad before they even tell me. I can feel it when they walk in the door after school. Their sadness is a vibration that is streaming out from them and I tune into it. It will make me feel sad and, if I didn't know better, I might think that I am unexplainably sad all of a sudden. However, because I was feeling quite peaceful before they came in, I recognize that this new feeling is a vibration that I am tuning into and not my own. This is called empathic communication.

You don't even have to know the person to tap into what they are feeling. Think about the grocery store clerk. I know I always scan for the one that feels the happiest to me and steer clear of the ones that feel irritated about their job. We tune in constantly to people because we can't help it.

When we were children we relied on our skills of tuning in or feeling energy to keep us safe. I am sure you remember feeling when it was a good time to ask mom for something and when it was a good time to keep your mouth closed. If you ignored your interpretations of the environment you usually regretted it.

We are naturally made to tune into energy vibrations. We are all quite literally antennas that pick up the vibrations around us or directed at us from anywhere. Like miniature radio receivers, depending on what dial we have our tuner set at, we can pick up various forms of vibrations. We simply need to learn to set our internal tuner to pick up the vibrations we want to.

If you want to listen to your favorite radio station you know you have to set the dial to the right frequency. You don't just turn it on and hope it will be there, you have to physically adjust it to pick up what you want to hear. Likewise, if you want to pick up the vibrations of spirit you must set your internal dial to pick up those frequencies.

How do we tune into vibrations of spirit? How do we set the dial, so to speak, to the right stations? The answer is through our intention. Thought energy follows intention. So, if we intend to pick up on a particular frequency of energy, we will do so through our desire.

We can send thoughts and feelings to anyone, anywhere. Remember that field of energy that unites us all? It is infinite and has no time or space. It is everywhere at once. So we are linked to all things at all times! This is kind of like the instant messaging we see on our cell phones today.

Because we are in physical reality we have an illusion of separateness. We can imagine in this physical reality that there is a "me" and there is a "you". This is what makes it fun! So, with our intention, the "me" can focus on the "you" and experience what "you" are feeling, thinking, etc. and still also have the experience of "me-ness". The wonderful thing about this is that you can focus on someone who is no longer physical but still exists and is connected to you vibrationally through this Unified Field.

Just like your friend who picked up your thoughts before you called, your loved ones can pick up your thoughts that you are having about them. They also have the ability to send you thoughts. The difference between what you and what your loved ones do, is that they choose to send and receive their thoughts consciously. You, unaware of your ability to pick up these thoughts and feelings, think it's your imagination or your own thoughts and feelings.

So, all these years you've been a walking, talking receiver of vibrational information. You've been sending out vibrations and receiving vibrations. This is something every single one of us does.  We are all natural born empathic communicators- feelers of energy.

It is impossible to destroy energy and so thoughts and feelings are bouncing around us everywhere we go.  We can choose to listen and feel or ignore the signals around us.  It is up to us.  We can train ourselves to become better receivers and better senders of energy through practice and intention. You are going to find this to be the most important tool you have in being a medium.

# Chapter 3

## Picking up the Vibes

*"I am convinced that there are universal currents of Divine Thought vibrating the ether everywhere and that any who can feel these vibrations is inspired."*
*Richard Wagner- German Composer*

Even though death removes the physical body the spiritual body continues to exist. Remember, energy cannot be destroyed! It is this spiritual body that we can learn to perceive. Mediums are persons who have learned how to pick up the vibrations of spirit and to interpret them. They can tune into the vibrations of those who are physical and those who are not.

There are various vibrations that mediums can tune into: thoughts, feelings, smells, physical sensations and gut feelings. In this chapter, we'll discover how you may interpret these vibrations yourself.

Thought vibrations can be perceived in two ways- words or images. The medium sets their intention to keep their minds clear and open, thinking no thoughts of their own. It is important to keep your own thoughts quiet in order to know that what you are receiving is from someone else.

Meditation is the most effective way to create this quiet mind (we will discuss meditation in Chapter 5).

Thoughts sent by spirits will come in two ways: pictures in your mind or words. You will need to be able to pay focused attention on everything that comes into your mind.

Pictures may come into your mind when you are open to vibrations of spirit. These pictures may be like a scene in your head playing out like a movie or may be simplistic like symbols. I have a list of the symbols I receive from spirit to indicate particular things (see Appendix A).

The symbols will come into your mind like a flash and be gone. So, sharp attention is imperative to your success. You will get used to certain images meaning certain things with practice. This will make the communications quicker for you over time.

If they send you a memory it will appear as a scene playing out- like watching a movie or possibly being in the scene yourself (this can be difficult to tolerate when the scene is unpleasant). If you have ever seen the TV show Medium on NBC, this is how the main character Allison receives most of her information. The information you receive will look exactly like when you use your imagination to see something and can even be accompanied by emotions.

Because it seems to be coming from inside of you, and not from someone else, most people will shrug it off as unimportant. Most people are already getting information from their loved ones in the forms of dreams or memory flash backs. They simply shrug it off as their own longings and do not realize someone is trying to say "hello".

It is your intention to receive information from spirit that makes the pictures worth paying attention to. Your intention to communicate is an invitation to spirit to speak to your mind. So, mediums will set their intention to speak to spirit and then trust everything that comes to them because of this intention.

Thoughts can also be received as an internal voice or words. This is called clairaudience, which literally means clear hearing. It will seem like your own voice inside of your head.

When another psychic told me that I was clairaudient, I disagreed with her. I told her, "I don't hear any voices". I assumed that I would hear those voices of spirit externally, like a voice out of thin air. She explained to me that the voices are heard internally, and sound much like my own with the difference being that I would hear the voices when I wasn't thinking about anything- when my mind was empty. Needless to say, this was happening to me all the time!

It became important for me to learn to tell the difference between my own thoughts and those I was receiving from spirit. I am not saying that you cannot hear the voices externally, you may. It's just much easier to tune into them internally and definitely not as frightening! Anyone who has heard their name called out from thin air can testify to the chills that run up the spine.

During one of my first healing sessions, I was working on a young woman with breast cancer when I received the image of a man in a flannel shirt standing at the end of the massage table. I could see him smile and nod at me and then he was gone.

This came like a flash and was followed by the word "lumberjack" in my mind. Now, being from Missouri, lumberjacks were only something I had heard about in stories, like Paul Bunyan. So, I was very doubtful of what I had just received. I took a deep breath and I released my doubt.

I decided to tell the client what I had just seen and heard. She gasped and started crying, saying "That's my grandfather! He was a lumberjack and he died of cancer."

I was stunned and emotional when I heard the words "your strength" come into my mind along with a feeling in my body of love and tenderness for the client. I shared all of this with her and watched as she cried tears of gratitude.

Feelings, or emotions, are also vibrations a medium may tune into. When a spirit sends emotional vibrations out to you, you will feel them as your own. When my client's grandfather sent feelings of love and tenderness to her, I felt them in my own body. I could see she was feeling them too.

Just like the mind must be clear to receive the thought vibrations of spirit, so must the heart be clear to feel the emotional vibrations of spirit. Having the heart be clear is also achieved through meditation, experiencing only the vibration of peace and calmness within you.

Having a foundational place of peace within you allows you, with your intention, to tune into the emotional vibrations of spirit. These emotional vibrations, like the thought vibrations, **will feel like your own**. Your awareness that they are not your own, because of your intention to feel peace and calmness, is what makes the difference in how you interpret them.

These feelings may come quickly and pass quickly, so paying close attention to what you feel is important when communicating with spirit. When you feel the emotions, acknowledge them and let them go.

Feeling vibrations of spirit can be anything we feel as humans. Even though they are in a place of love and peace, they may communicate feelings of sadness and remorse about the way they passed. This is especially common if they took their own life or caused their own passing through negligent behavior.

One thing I will stress is that this does not mean this spirit is in a negative place or feeling those negative emotions constantly. It simply is a communication of feeling about the way they passed- a way to say, "I am sorry" with their heart, not just with words.

When I mention how the spirit is feeling, the client may feel this in their body too. This can be very healing for them. This is called sympathetic vibration. It is important to acknowledge so the client can have a "real" experience of their loved one, too.

One thing I have discovered is souls who have taken their own life go into a state of Peace with God after passing. However, they experience the effect of their death on their loved ones and this can create a feeling of remorse for them that they want communicated. Once this is shared a feeling of tremendous relief and peace usually follows.

Oddly enough, sometimes spirits will communicate through our sense of smell. You may get a faint whiff of pipe smoke or the smell of a familiar perfume. I had one spirit give me the most wonderful aroma of baked goods and cinnamon. I also got a picture of an odd shaped cookie with this aroma and told my client what I was smelling and seeing. She recognized this as a cookie her Polish grandmother used to bake with her every Christmas. The aroma was so strong my mouth was watering.

Spirits will sometimes try to get our attention by giving us a hint of their perfume or tobacco that we would associate with their presence. Do not underestimate these vibrations, they can be almost overpowering! My mother has this gift very strongly developed. She says she knows when her mother is around because she smells roses.

I may also tune into physical vibrations in my body. I will receive physical sensations in my body to indicate how a person passed such as chest pain, or difficulty breathing. This can sometimes be a little uncomfortable, but if you ask the spirit you are speaking with to "lighten up a little" they will always do so.

Physical sensations can be strong or gentle. I may feel heavy pressure in my chest, a light tapping sensation on my forehead, or even a gentle pressure in my lower abdomen. I have to pay very close attention to any sensations I feel.

As I practiced my new skill of mediumship, I discovered that even though I was speaking with new spirits each session they would consistently use the same sensations in my body to communicate with me (see Appendix B). These same feelings would indicate different ways of passing, such as disease or trauma.

When you begin interpreting signals in your body it may be a little challenging. If you ever feel confused about what you are sensing in your body, simply describe the sensations exactly and pay attention to any thoughts that come with the sensations.

I have a nursing background, so I know where the internal organs are located, etc. If you don't, it might help you to get a basic overview of where your major organs are in your body, such as your kidneys, pancreas and liver.

Your body, like your mind and heart, will need to be in a calm, pain free place to be able to clearly detect physical vibration signals. If you have a headache or aches and pains of any kind, it's better to wait until you feel better so you aren't confused.

Finally, the most powerful vibration you may tune into is your gut instinct or inner knowing. If you haven't developed faith in your gut instinct, you won't have much luck being a medium. There are many times where this is the only signal you are getting clearly and you need to be able to put your faith in it 100%.

You may get a sensation that you don't understand or a symbol comes to mind you don't recognize. This is when you will need to "go with your gut" and trust what you feel the meaning is. This is how I learned to interpret all the symbols and sensations I share with you at the back of this book.

I still receive new symbols and sensations for me to figure out when I do readings. It's kind of like God is trying to expand my spiritual vocabulary. The only way to develop this ability is to be patient and have faith in yourself.

**Chapter 4**

**Becoming a Medium- The Process**

*"The most beautiful thing we can experience is the mysterious. It is the source of all true art and science. He to whom this emotion is a stranger, who can no longer pause to wonder and stand rapt in awe, is as good as dead: his eyes are closed"*
*Albert Einstein (1879-1955)*

So, now that you know the different vibrational languages or ways in which spirit may communicate with you, how do you use this knowledge to become a medium? There are 5 steps that I go through each time I connect with spirit: asking, opening, receiving, giving and gratitude.

Asking for the communication is a crucial step in the process. By asking for spirit to speak to us we are declaring our intention. This is like prayer! You cannot receive what you do not ask for. Notice that I said, ask not demand. You want to approach the process with reverence for the souls you will be contacting. They are not obligated to communicate, although it is rare that they do not want to.

Usually, if a soul doesn't communicate it is because there is another soul who desires the time with me. I do suggest that my clients pray before coming to a session and personally ask the souls they want to speak with to show up. Ninety-nine percent of the time they do.

So, asking, being the first step in the process, is simply to state your intention to connect with those on the other side who would like to speak with you today. You can do this internally or out loud.

You may also request a particular person by asking for them by name. Remember, the universal field that connects us all will get the message to them instantly. It's kind of like our new cell phone technology with Instant Messaging! They hear your request and will usually send you a "warm fuzzy" to let you know they heard you.

Secondly, we must clear our minds, hearts and body with meditation and become open to the communication. Once you establish a meditation practice you will easily be able to be in this open peaceful state with a few simple deep breaths. For me, this feels like becoming empty and calm. The more relaxed you are the easier it will be to move to the next step, which is receiving.

Almost immediately I will begin to receive information by paying attention to everything I think, see in my mind, feel in my body and feel in my heart emotionally. This requires trust. I trust everything I get to be a communication. I know that I can trust it because I established the open empty space within my body, heart and mind and I set an intention to communicate with spirit. Everything I receive will be from spirit.

The next step is giving. I either give to myself or to the client, depending if I am alone or doing a reading for someone else. Giving to myself, would consist of allowing myself to believe in what I am receiving and feeling the love my loved one is offering to me. I must believe that I deserve this communication to allow that love into my experience. For me the experience is like feeling a warm hug, an overwhelming love and acceptance, and hearing "I love you" in my mind.

I do not allow myself to destroy this gift by doubting it! I receive the love and listen to the words that come into my mind. I allow myself to ask questions I am seeking guidance on and allow myself to receive the answers in words, pictures, feelings or inner knowing. This is how I give to myself.

If I am doing a reading for another person, my giving to them consists of sharing everything I receive. I try not to leave anything out. Sometimes the information comes quicker than I can share but I just keep trusting it and give it all to them. I leave nothing out! This requires you to have humility.

You must let go of any need you have to be right! If you allow your ego to give the reading, everything you receive in the form of vibrations will be doubted and questioned. This will cause you to feel uncomfortable and embarrassed. If you find yourself feeling that way during a reading you let your ego get involved.

Finally, when you have allowed yourself to receive what you needed or you have given the client all the information you received for them let yourself become grateful. Gratitude is the last step of the process.

I allow myself to come back to the place of peace and calmness I began with and I begin to say "Thank you" over and over until my heart is full of gratitude. This gratitude tells God that I liked this communication and would like "more please" in the future. We always get more of what we are grateful for.

# Chapter 5

## Tools for Expanding the Gift

*"There is nothing as disobedient as an undisciplined mind, and there is nothing as obedient as a disciplined mind."*
***The Buddha***

Meditation, faith in your ability to trust your imagination and gratitude are the most important tools you have for expanding the gift of spirit communication. If you simply focus your attention on developing these areas you will succeed!

Meditation is an ancient practice of calming the mind, body and emotions. This practice needs to be done on a daily basis to be effective. It consists of focusing all of your attention on the breath and becoming a detached witness to the mind, body and emotions. Read the following paragraph and then try the practice on your own.

Always make sure you are alone and will not be disturbed before attempting meditation. I use earplugs and a blindfold if I need to. This helps me to really go deep inside of my self.

Sit upright comfortably supported. Set a timer for 10 minutes (once you have mastered this skill you may extend your time).

Close your eyes and focus on your breathing. Feel the air entering and leaving your body. Do not attempt to control your breath, simply watch it and feel it. If any thoughts come into your mind only notice them and let them go. Do not allow them to carry you away from your focus on your breath.

Continue this process for the full 10 minutes. Allow whatever feeling may arise in your body to rise up and witness them as you let them go. Keep your intention on emptiness and stillness. Let your breath carry all thoughts and feelings out with your exhales.

At first, you may be surprised how difficult it is to quiet your mind and keep your attention only on your breath! This is why daily practice is so important. As you do this practice your mind will become obedient to your spirit, which is the part of you that was doing the watching.

If your mind is quiet than so will your emotions become quiet and finally your body. This can take several sessions to experience mind, body and heart stillness. So, be patient and persistent. You will need to have this skill mastered to be able to be a clear medium.

Faith in your imagination is where most people find their greatest challenge. They ask to talk to their loved ones and begin to tune into the communications. Then feeling the love and seeing an image of their loved one in their mind they say, "Who am I kidding? This is just my imagination. It isn't real." And by doing this, they slam the door on their loved ones communication and create a big feeling of disappointment inside of themselves. Why? Probably, because someone told them at sometime in their life that their imagination wasn't something to trust.

Now, I know the imagination can get away from us sometimes and create some very unrealistic pictures that, if we allowed ourselves to believe in, would probably cause us a trip to the insane asylum. Letting our imaginations run wild is letting our subconscious minds control us. That is not what I am talking about. I am talking about using the imagination with intention, in teamwork with our conscious minds!

In order to communicate with spirit, we must link our imagination with our conscious mind and use it as a tool. In this case, trusting it is imperative to our success.

The imagination is our ability to connect with other realms of reality, its true purpose. If you want to communicate with your loved ones, you will have to let go of your doubts about your imagination's power. You will need to create a place in your imagination that they can come to you and visit with you.

Your imagination is the doorway to heaven. Remember Jesus said, "Ye must be as little children to enter the kingdom of heaven". This is because children believe in and understand the power of their imaginations! So, before you proceed further, make a decision right now to be willing to believe you can trust your imagination. It is the door to the kingdom. If you cannot, then you may as well stop reading. If you won't walk through the doorway to heaven, you'll never get inside.

Gratitude is the tool that will guarantee your gift will expand. What you are grateful for God always gives you more of. So, in the beginning of your practice, be grateful for every little vibration you pick up on. This will guarantee you will receive more. Excitement about the communications translates to gratitude in God's eyes.

When I first began receiving communications I would get so excited and my heart would race. I wanted to do it all the time! I loved this new skill and appreciated anything I could tune into. I was so grateful for it that I promised myself I would trust it and act on it no matter what. God took me up on that!

I found myself one evening sitting at a Chinese restaurant with my husband during a Wisconsin snowstorm. We were the only customers in the whole place when an elderly gentleman walked in covered in snow. I felt an instant pull to him.

I began to receive feelings of sadness and overwhelming loneliness. I heard in my mind, "his wife is dying". I felt so distressed by what I was receiving that I couldn't eat.

I shared with my husband what I was experiencing. He turned to look at the gentleman who was smiling and flirting with the waitress at his table. "He looks fine to me" he said as he turned back around. "Yes, you're probably right", I said, trying to pick up my fork and begin eating again.

No matter what I did, I couldn't shake the feelings I was having. I could actually feel an inner urge pushing me to get up and go to his table. I dug my heels deep into the carpet. I was staying put!

Finally, after unrelenting feelings of "help him", I came up with a compromise. "I'll tell you what", I said internally. "I'll tell him what I am feeling if you get him to come to me". I smiled satisfied that I had just gotten myself out of an uncomfortable situation.

As we finished our meal and got up to leave the man approached us. I felt my stomach turn over in fear. "Here we go", I thought to myself. He asked us if we could give him a ride just across the street where his car was being worked on. My husband smiled and looked at me, knowing his part was to say "yes". I smiled back and felt a warmth come over my body.

After I climbed into the back seat to allow the gentleman a comfortable seat in front, I reached forward and put my hands on his heart. Startled, he looked at me. With tears in my eyes I spoke. "There is an angel with you and she says not to worry about your wife. She will not be alone. They will be with her and will make sure she is ok."

His shoulders began to shake and tears fell as he thanked me for sharing this information with me. He told us how his wife was dying from cancer this very minute at a nursing home and how he couldn't get to her because of his car breaking down. Something had told him to go to the restaurant across the street while he waited for the mechanics to fix his car.

We waited for a few minutes to let him calm down and then I watched as my husband squeezed his hand. No more words were needed. I fell back in gratitude for what had just happened.

I was so grateful that I could be a vessel of comfort to someone at such a horrible time. Now I understand that the gratitude I felt that night was my prayer asking for more opportunities to give. They came by the hundreds! So, make gratitude a firm part of your practicing and you will be guaranteed to receive more opportunities to feel grateful.

# Chapter 6

## Connecting with Your Own Loved Ones

*"You read the face of the sky and of the earth, but you have not recognized the one who is before you, and you do not know how to read this moment" - The Gospel of Thomas from the Nag Hammadi Library*

Connecting with your own loved ones is much easier than connecting to the loved ones of others. The love that you feel for each other is a power that overcomes any boundary you may feel is between you. That love is like a constant invitation to them to be with you. It gives them permission to be close to you and to share their vibrations with you.

Even though you don't perceive them physically anymore, they are still here. They will let you know in vibrational ways (the language of spirit) they are with you: thoughts, feelings, smells and sensations. So, you must pay attention to those signals.

The first step is to ask. So ask! Ask them to be with you and talk to you. If you have someone in particular that you want to speak with ask them personally to come to you. You may ask out loud or inside. It doesn't matter.

Remember thoughts are vibrations that can be felt by spirit, too. They will hear you.

Next, is to open. This is where your meditation skills will come into play. Focus on your breath and let go. Feel peace and calm. Deeply relax your mind and body. The next few paragraphs contain a meditation exercise that I created for connecting with loved ones. Read through it once before attempting. If you prefer listening to someone take you through the meditation, there is an order form at the back of the book for an audio CD that will guide you through this exercise.

Make sure you have at least 20 minutes where you will not be disturbed. Sit with your eyes closed and be willing to receive information. Have a pencil and pad of paper to record whatever you receive. Say a prayer if you'd like and invite your loved ones to spend time with you.

Now take several deep breaths and imagine each and every muscle of your body relaxing deeply and letting go. Scan through your entire body, beginning with your feet and moving upwards. Feel if there are any areas that need to be relaxed a little more. If there are, use your exhale to imagine letting the tension leave through your breath. Take your time on this step. Relaxation is very important for quieting the body.

When you feel deeply relaxed, imagine in your mind an elevator door. See and feel yourself stepping inside of this elevator. You will be selecting the number 8. This is for the 8th Chakra located about 12 inches above your head. You are currently on the "B" floor for body.

Imagine the elevator beginning to move upwards into floor 1 and see the color red filling the elevator. Feel this color in your body moving from the head downwards through your feet.

Next move up to floor 2 and see the color orange coming downwards into your body. Feel it entering the crown of your head and moving downwards through your feet.

As you move up to floor 3, feel and see a warm yellow light coming downwards and warming your body. Let it pass downwards and through your feet.

Then feel yourself moving upwards to floor 4 and see the color green coming into your body. Smell the green of grass and feel this color flooding your body and moving out your feet.

Next, move upwards to Floor 5. Imagine a beautiful cobalt blue entering the top of the elevator and washing down through your body. Feel its healing qualities as it cleanses you and passes through the floor.

As you move up and into floor 6 you experience the color violet or indigo (a purplish-blue color). Let this colors enter in through the top of your head and feel the front of your forehead relaxing. This is the color that activates your spiritual vision, your imagination. Allow it to pass downwards and through your feet.

On floor 7 allow a deep purple to fill your body or if you prefer a lavender. Breathe it into the top of your head and then allow it to gently pass through your cells and body into the floor of the elevator.

Next, move slowly in your imagination upwards out of the purple into a brilliant white light. Even in your imagination your eyes may feel slightly uncomfortable as you adjust to this brightness. Feel yourself lifted into this beautiful light.

See the white light in and around every cell of your body. Let yourself imagine that you are beginning to glow! Feel a humming in all of your cells. Let your face begin to tingle slightly as the light activates your body. Sit in this light for a while.

Feel the stillness of this light. Feel the purity and peace of this light and let it embrace you and love you. This light is love.

Next allow your imagination to create a place in this light for your loved one to come spend time with you. Create a beautiful garden with flowers, water and birds if you like. Take time to add the details. Smell the flowers and hear the animals that you have placed here.

Spend a little time on this! You may have a place that you and your loved one spent a lot of time together, or a place you both loved to visit. Include a place to sit down and talk in your garden.

When creating this place use all of your five senses in your imagination. See the scene, smell the scene, hear birds or water in the scene, touch the flowers or grass, and take a drink of water or chew a blade of grass to open up your sense of taste. This will activate your full being and full awareness.

Then breathe into your heart and open your heart by feeling love for the person you want to communicate with. Let yourself remember them as much as you can. Then trust and wait.

Usually when a spirit comes to you, you will feel a sensation physically that they are near you. This can be an inner knowing or tingles may be felt in your body. I will feel a fullness in my heart. My chest may actually feel a little tight from the opening of my heart. Trust this and feel gratitude for the sensations or awareness.

If you would like, you can allow your imagination to invite a visual experience of the person. "See" them approaching you in this beautiful place. Let yourself see an image of them in your mind. Create it as vivid as you can. This is using your imagination with your conscious mind.

They will co-create this with you, so don't be surprised if they look different than the last time you saw them! They may appear younger, healthier and happier to you. Just let it be whatever it is.

If you'd like, go and sit on the bench or seat you created in your garden. This will become a sacred place for you each time you come here. Don't be surprised if the next time you attempt the meditation, someone is already waiting there for you!

If you don't get a visual of the person, ask for a name to come into your mind. A lot of the time the name will "pop in" before you even finish the sentence or you will just have a gut feeling as to whom this person is. Trust everything you receive and continue to feel grateful each time you receive something.

Say "Hello" to them internally and offer them love from your heart, if you desire. This is usually very easy because when you see them your heart bursts with love and remembering. Most of the time tears will come with this remembering.

45

You may begin to feel your heart opening and sometimes an overwhelming sense of love will overpower you. Let it happen. They are triggering your feelings of missing them, which is really love that has been held in place with nowhere to go. Perhaps, you hadn't realized you could keep loving them and giving love to them and so you hold it back in your heart, which creates an ache we call 'missing them'.

Let it all go, cry if you need. Just pour all that love and ache out to them. You will reach a place of relief and then communication can begin.

Allow yourself to have an internal conversation with them. Ask them how they are doing and let yourself hear a response or feel an answer with your inner knowing. It's ok to write down whatever they say to you. You can always close your eyes and go back inside.

Ask them if there is anything they want you to know. Listen and allow the response to come. Perhaps they will surprise you with something you didn't expect and then you will know they are truly with you.

I was doing this meditation once and when I arrived off of the elevator I noticed a mailbox in my garden. I hadn't put that there! It had the little red flag up on it, indicating there was mail inside waiting to be delivered. I walked over to it and opened the door. There was a letter inside!

As I pulled the letter out, I could feel the excitement in my body. I hadn't anticipated any of this. Someone was surprising me. When I opened the letter it said "I love you" and the name of someone very special to me was signed at the bottom. So, be open to anything happening and have a good time with it.

When you see your loved one, imagine that you can touch them and feel them again. Imagine them hugging you. This can be so powerful! If you need to, see yourself crying on their shoulder. Just allow your imagination to work for you. I have allowed myself to hug a pillow just to give my body the physical sensations it wants.

Our loved ones like to touch our shoulders and our cheeks frequently. You may feel pressure on your shoulder or a slight breeze on your cheek.

Many times, on the first attempt at connecting with a loved one, we are simply overwhelmed by emotion. We just need to let all that grief come up and get out of our way. Before you can have a clear communication, all of these heavier emotions have to be out of the way.

You may even have old feelings of anger come up for you if there are unresolved issues with a loved one. Or perhaps, this was a much unexpected loss and the grief is still very raw for you. In this case, the communication can be a little tougher because there is so much emotion in the way.

Be patient with yourself and allow whatever you are feeling. You may need to speak your truth about your anger or disappointments if you have them. Go ahead and say whatever you need to. Your loved one can take it!

One thing I know for sure is that they want to offer you comfort. If you have been suffering greatly from their passing, they know this and want to help. Let them.

I have had many souls communicate to me during sessions that the clients they were here to see were here for "unfinished business". The client usually had feelings of anger or confusion about their loved one's passing or their loved one was abusive to them when they were alive and they needed some closure or understanding about what had happened.

When a soul passes they experience what some refer to as a "life review". During this life review process, they experience the effects of their actions on others as if they were the person they harmed or helped. So, when they come to apologize or explain themselves during a session, I know they are speaking from a total understanding of their actions.

So, if you have unresolved issues with a soul who has crossed, this is the perfect time to speak your mind and express your truth. Just be willing to feel your feelings too! Let this be a complete healing for yourself if you can.

After you say whatever you need to your loved one, sit and allow any communications they may want to share with you. Even though you may have a hundred questions you want to ask them, take it slow.

The connection will get clearer and clearer each time you do it. I have had many students tell me that on their first attempt they could see their loved one but couldn't hear anything from them. That's ok, with time and practice you will learn to allow it. As you let go of your resistance to hearing them, the telepathic receiving on your part will open up.

Your loved ones are patient and will wait for you to trust. If you have trouble hearing them the first time, just allow yourself to enjoy seeing them and feeling their love.

On a rare occasion I have had students that couldn't allow the image of their loved one into their mind. In this case, I instruct them to find a picture of the person they most want to see and focus on that. Soon the picture will be able to be held inside the mind. It just requires a little patience and practice.

One thing I must point out is that your loved ones aren't here to give you answers to "what should I do" questions. They know the best thing is to let you discover your own answers in life. They also aren't going to give you future predictions like lottery numbers or race horses. Although, this is simply based on my own experience. If you run across someone who has had a different experience, please let me know!

After you have spent as much time as you'd like with your loved one, kiss and hug them goodbye for now. Then let yourself move back to the elevator. Step inside and push the "B" button for body.

Feel yourself descending down into your body. Take it as slow as you need. See the numbers as you move downwards 8,7,6,5,4,3,2,1 then B. When you feel solid and grounded, open your eyes.

Say a prayer of thank you until your heart feels full of gratitude. Your loved one will feel it. Remind yourself you can come back to this experience anytime you choose. Just knowing you can come back will help you to be calmer and clearer each time.

I recommend, in the beginning, setting aside time once a week to connect. I don't recommend more than that. Of course, it isn't going to harm you to do more. It simply needs to not keep you from focusing on the other areas of your life.

You are alive for a reason! You have things to do here. So, don't get carried away with hanging out in heaven with your loved ones so much it keeps you from doing what you need to do in physical reality.

To assist you in connecting with your own loved ones, I have a guided meditation audio CD. It will walk you through relaxing and help you to open your inner vision. To purchase it go to **http://www.martinaschmidt.com**

## Chapter 7

## Being a Medium for Others

*"Love is the light that dissolves all walls between souls,
families and nations."*
*Paramahansa Yogananda*

If you find that you enjoy communicating with your loved ones and would like to expand your skills to help others you can do so with practice. Ask anyone who is willing to let you practice on them to sit for a reading.

Once you get better at your skill you won't have to ask anymore, they will all come to you. I found people more than willing to let me try my skills out on them. Because they know you are practicing they are usually very patient and happy to give you feedback.

The steps taken in doing a reading for another person are the same ones to connect with your own loved ones: asking, opening, receiving, giving and gratitude. If I can, I like to have the client say a prayer before coming and ask whomever they wish to speak with to be present at the session. This is the client's asking part.

Before a client arrives for a reading I do my meditation practice. It can be nerve wracking when you first do sessions because you are so worried about doing it wrong. So, meditation to calm your nerves as much as possible is very important.

Just sit and breathe with the intention of feeling only peace and calm in your body and mind. I will do this for at least 10 minutes before my client's arrive.

When the client arrives for the reading, I will have them sit directly in front of me. I close my eyes and calm myself. I do my asking by saying internally, "I ask anyone who would like to communicate with us today for our highest good to do so now." You could also speak this out loud if you'd like. With this intention, I know I am only asking those souls who have our best interest at heart to be present.

Next I simply breathe and relax to open myself. I become empty and willing to receive. Almost immediately I will be **drawn** to a particular location near the client. Notice I said drawn. My attention and my eyes will want to look at a specific area around the client in front of me. I have learned that there are specific locations our loved ones will stand next to us to indicate how they are related to us and whether they are male or female.

I am grateful to say, that every soul on the other side somehow knows this standard of operation. It makes it much easier when you can count on them to follow a few rules.

I believe, because we are all connected by the unified field, they have access to all of my memories, etc. So, by memorizing the charts and symbols I have provided you with in the back of this book, you will have guidelines for them to follow.

So, again, the first thing I identify is if they are male/female. Males will come in on the right side of the client and females on the left (see Appendix C). Depending on how they are related to the client, they will either come in above the client if they are older, at the shoulder level if they are the same generation, or around elbow level of the client if they are younger.

Children of the client will usually come in around the lap area of the person. If they are not the client's child but are a younger generation they will come in around the elbow area.

Pets will usually come in as a sensation around your ankle area. I have had dogs, cats, horses, birds, and rabbits come in to say hello! Thank goodness no one has had a snake or mouse come through to communicate. I am not sure how happy I would be to convey that message! Horses being bigger, however, will try to send you an image of a horse in your mind rather than tapping at your ankle (thank goodness).

The oddest pet I have had come during a reading was a rabbit! It just sat in my lap like a silver ball of fluff. It wouldn't give me words or feelings. It just sat there quiet. I kept telling the client, "I think I have a pet here but I am so unsure because it just feels like a quiet ball of silver fluff." The client had recently lost her grey rabbit, who she had named Fluffy. So this was very significant and healing for her!

After I have identified the sex of the person and their possible relationship to the client I will begin to receive physical sensations in my own body that indicate how the person passed (see Appendix B). These can be very clear or very subtle and difficult to understand. Such as, I feel heaviness and pain in the back of my heart, right around the middle of my back, when someone has passed from a heart attack. It can actually feel a little uncomfortable.

If someone passed on cancer I will feel two things: a sensation in my right armpit (the lymph node area) and also sensations in the area the cancer originated in. So, I may feel pressure in my armpit and also in the area of my pancreas.

If I am feeling a new sensation that I don't recognize then I simply describe what I am feeling and where I am feeling the sensation in my body. The client will usually understand what this means or can connect it to symptoms their loved one experienced before passing.

Patience is the key. If you don't understand something a spirit is trying to tell you then ask them to give you something else to help you have clarity. Wait, listen and pay attention to everything you feel.

You will get used to the sensations spirits use to communicate. I have included a list in the back of this book for you to refer to for the most common sensations you may feel to indicate ways of passing (see Appendix B).

After giving the means of passing, I begin to receive thoughts from the spirit. I may get pictures that flash into my mind or I may see numbers or a letter of the alphabet. I will sometimes hear a word or name in my mind.

Names can be tricky because of the quickness they are received. So, it is always best to make the exact sounds you hear if the name isn't recognized. The name Patricia and Theresa sound exactly alike when you say them as a quick whisper. You'll get used to the way certain names sound with practice but it's best to just sound them out loud.

If you have trouble with the sound of a name, ask them to simply give you the first letter of the name and allow a letter of the alphabet to come into your mind.

If they flash a number into your mind this usually indicates a month or day of the month that is significant to them, such as day of passing or birthday. Always have the client take note of the date, as most of us don't remember off the top of our heads all of our loved ones exact dates of passing!

On a rare occasion a number will mean how many children the spirit had. I remember the first time a client asked me to have her father tell me how many children he had. When the number 9 came into my head I was doubtful of my accuracy. I gave the information anyways and was glad to find out it was correct. He followed the 9 with the letter "J". All nine of his children had "J" names!

Remember that spirits also have access to your memory banks. So, if you see an image of your Aunt Sally come into your mind, give the name Sally to the client or ask what it is about Aunt Sally they want you to remember. It could be that she was a famous musician and this spirit was also a famous musician. You will have to trust your gut instinct on these types of communications. My father-in-law was a fireman and so if he comes into my mind I know the spirit I am communicating with was a fireman.

With all of the information you will be receiving there may be moments when you feel confused or the client seems confused. In this situation, go back to your calm place and relax. Ask for clarity if you feel you are misunderstanding something. Do not rush yourself, especially in the beginning when you are learning.

Sometimes, you will have to just trust what you feel inside of you to be true. This can be challenging for us when we have learned to put so much faith in the external world.

I have had clients who get what I call "psychic amnesia" and will stare at me blankly when I give them information. They will shake their heads confused about what I am saying. This can be frustrating and make you want to throw in the towel. Don't give up! They are simply nervous from this very uncommon situation of having a reading.

In this situation I will close my eyes and go inside to see what my inner knowing says to me. If I feel like maybe I am not quite on target, I will breathe, relax and start over. It is always ok to say, "Let me try again". Being accurate is most important, not looking good to the client.

Many times when I start over I will feel "yes this is correct information". It's like a feeling of absolute confidence in what I have received. If the client is still unsure then I will tell them to write down what I have told them to research at a later time. It is very common for the client to call or email me later to tell me the information was correct after all.

Sadly I had a young man named Paul, who had committed suicide, come through during a reading I had done with his Aunt. I gave her his name, how he passed and even told her this was a younger male, possibly a nephew. She kept shaking her head saying she didn't know who I was talking about. I asked her to write down the information and then I let go and moved on to someone else.

Several days after her reading I received a phone call from her. She was in tears. After she had gotten home she remembered an estranged nephew named Paul who had hung himself several years ago. She was very distressed when she realized who she had forgotten.

Paul's mother (my client's sister-in-law) and my client hadn't seen each other for quite some time. When she remembered who he was, she picked up the phone and called her sister-in-law to tell her about the reading. This was a wonderful reunion for both of them.

She then called me to tell me how sorry she was and asked if I could give Paul, her forgotten nephew, her apologies. I reminded her that Paul was already aware of everything that had transpired and that he was grateful she had reached out to his mother.

Another incident where client amnesia occurred, I was doing a group reading for 150 people and had come to an elderly woman with her 2 daughters. I looked at the woman and began to read for her.

I said "I feel the presence of a male with you and he is giving me the letter R. She shook her head and said nothing. I continued, "He is showing me a heart and that it belongs to you- so I feel like he may be your husband?" Again, she shook her head and said "NO".

My gut was telling me that I was getting clear and accurate information even though the face in front of me was completely confused. So, I stood there wondering what to do.

About this time, the young woman sitting next to her was squirming excitedly in her seat. I looked at her hoping she could help and she blurted out, "Mother, dad's name started with an R!" At this moment, the elderly woman's face became very red and she said, "Oh my goodness, I can't believe I forgot that!"

After further inquiry, I discovered that her husband's name was Richard and that everyone had called him by his nickname, Dick. She had been so nervous by my presence that she completely shut that information out. Seems impossible sometimes, I know, but it still happens.

It can be frustrating to encounter a client who is forgetful, but it certainly will happen. Because the nature of the work is slightly frightening for some people, you will have to be patient and as calming as you can be. If you know a client is afraid, then talk their fears over with them first to help them calm down and be ready. Humor is a great way to help people open and relax.

Sometimes clients will create a list of names of everyone they know that has passed and bring it with them to their session. This can be extremely helpful. Just make sure they keep it hidden from you!

Because you will never know if someone is simply forgetting their loved one or if you are misunderstanding the communications coming in, you will need to develop a strong gut instinct. If you want to be a great medium, you will need to put your greatest faith in your internal messages first, not what the client says.

This gut instinct may also help you to feel if the person you are describing and the person the client feels you may be speaking to are one and the same. Sometimes, a client wants to hear from their loved one so badly they will try to mold and shape what you are saying to fit who they want to speak to.

If you feel you're talking about two different people and it isn't whom they were seeking, then you will need to gently let them know you are feeling this to be someone else. Give them a few moments and keep providing the details, their memories will come back to them as to who you are picking up on. Once they identify this other person, the one they were hoping for usually steps in.

I believe when a person makes an appointment to come and see a medium there is a bulletin board in heaven that lets everybody know. I have seen people come for a reading and their co-worker's father who just died comes through and their husband's whole family and maybe even their best friend's mother, but very few of their own family shows up. I cannot explain why this is, hence my bulletin board idea, which its more humor than fact. But, nonetheless, the word got out and unexpected souls showed up.

For whatever reason, I do know that whoever most needs to get through will. The clients that have the extraneous visitors usually are very much at peace with their own family members passing and just wanted to see what it was like to have a reading. So, Heaven efficiently uses the opportunity to get a few messages delivered through this willing soul to others who need it.

As you receive the information you offer it to the client. This is the giving step. **You must give everything you receive without analyzing it or changing it**. The smallest detail could mean the most to someone, so give it the way it comes in.

The most embarrassing moments for me have been some of the most grateful moments of my clients. Because I was willing to say exactly what I heard or describe exactly what I was seeing the information had the impact it was meant to have.

I have had spirits say things like, "Can you believe they let me in the door?" or even use profanity to express a point.

In this case I usually hint at the word or spell it out for them, rosy cheeks and all. So, keep your ego out of the picture and trust everything you receive as having a meaning and share it.

I have even had spirits give me words in another language! How silly I felt sounding out words I had never heard before. One of my clients had an uncle come through from Poland. He had invented a device and the family was trying to figure out what it was for. She asked me to ask him and a very strange word popped into my head. I cannot for the life of me remember what that word was, but I can tell you it meant "poppy seeds" in Polish.

The client knew exactly what I was saying. She told me how the family had been debating over the intended use of his invention but that most believed it was for grinding poppy seeds! This foreign word for me had given her the exact answer she was seeking.

Another client's father, whose was from Bulgaria, told me during a session to tell his daughter a word that sounded like "neeshka" and to point from his heart to hers. She told me the word meant "string" and knew full well the meaning he was conveying to her.

I had a young boy say "I love you" in German to his father. His father had asked him to give him this code when he came to see me so that he would know the reading wasn't a fake. When I spoke the foreign words of endearment, his father who had been very skeptical up to this point began to shout at me. "How did you know that? How did you know that?" He was so overtaken by grief mixed with gratitude that we had to end his session. Even though it was heart wrenching for him, I was glad I spoke the words I had heard. His son needed him to know he was still alive and well in Heaven. So, be adventurous and give everything you get, even if you don't understand it.

Trusting can be the hardest part for a medium. People don't like to make mistakes. They don't like to feel like a failure. So, rather than risking being wrong they just keep silent. I cannot stress enough how important it is that you don't censor what you are receiving. Stop trying to be right and get your ego out of the way. Some things can seem silly to you when you are receiving them and you may doubt that it is accurate information. Give it anyway!

Integrity and honesty are essential to having a clear reading. When you are thinking about being amazing or looking good to your client, you will interfere with the accuracy of the information coming through. Wanting to look good was my greatest obstacle. I wanted so much to help and be right that it created many challenges I had to overcome. Thank goodness, God is patient and I was able to learn to let go.

Be honest with yourself right now. Are you invested in gaining special attention for having these skills? If so examine those feelings in depth before you ever give a reading to another person.

I did a session over the phone for a client when I was first beginning. I was communicating with his grandfather and we had clearly gotten how he passed and his name. Next, I kept seeing a monkey flash in my mind. I thought to myself, "Oh and things were going so good until now. What is this crazy monkey doing in my head?"

My inner self reminded me of my decision to keep my ego out of the picture and so with nervousness, I told the man on the phone about the silly monkey in my mind. He began laughing to the point of tears.

I thought to myself, "Great! He thinks I'm nuts now." I was ready to hang up the phone when he gained his composure and said, "I can't believe he remembers that monkey!" I asked him to please explain and he began to share a heart-warming story. His grandfather had kept a little toy monkey on his bed. When my client was a little boy, he used to sneak in to his grandfather's bedroom and play with that monkey. He wasn't supposed to touch it because it was old and fragile, but to him it was irresistible! He had of course disobeyed on many occasions and obviously his grandfather was letting him know that he had known!

Along with your thoughts, pay attention to any emotions you may feel during a session. If you feel deep love then tell your client about it.  If you feel sadness then share this, too.  Just give it the way you are feeling it.  Someone may need to hear how sorry their father was for not being in their life.  You may not know why the spirit communicating to you is sending a feeling of being sorry, but you need to share it anyways.

I had a female client who came with her husband for a reading of her energy field.  She asked her husband to sit in the waiting area in case she needed him but that she wanted to have the reading done alone.  She had come to see me to discover the cause of a terminal illness she was battling.  She really wasn't looking for spirit communication but I had informed her of my gifts and that it was certainly a possibility during my scan of her.

When she sat down with me I immediately began to feel the presence of a man next to her.  I felt deep emotions of remorse and also a sense of pleading and urgency.  I began to describe these feelings to her.  She stared at me like a statue and didn't move.  What I heard next shocked me.

"I am her 3$^{rd}$ husband" the voice in my head shouted.  I looked at this woman confused, knowing her husband was in the waiting room. "Could she really have been married 4 times already?" I thought to myself.

The spirit repeated himself.  At this point I giggled with nervousness and said out loud, "I have a man here who desperately wants to talk to you and he is claiming to be your 3rd husband. Do you understand this?" Her expression began to change from stoic stillness to red faced rage. I backed up as she shouted, "What is he doing here? Tell him to get out of here. I never want to speak to him again!"

I continued calmly, "He wants to tell you he is sorry for leaving you and that your illness in your body is caused by your bitterness towards him. He's telling me he took his own life and that he was a coward to leave you behind. He's also telling me that he led someone named Ted to you. Who is Ted?" I asked.

"He's my current husband," she answered. "He's sitting in the waiting room." At this point, her face softened and she began to weep. "He left me with 4 children and no money. I'll never forgive him for killing himself."

I tried to explain the benefit of forgiveness to her and how it could help to heal her body. She told me she would rather die than forgive him. I sat there and watched as she thanked me for the information and got up to leave. There was nothing else I could do to help her. She was entitled to her bitterness, even if it was killing her to hold onto it.

When a spirit's emotions come through, it can be quite strong and you many need to ask them to ease off a little. I have felt moments where I wanted to cry and moments where I wanted to laugh. I like to say, "thank you I understand" and then I tell the soul who is communicating with me to stop sending the signals of emotion.

Towards the end of a session the signals and information will calm down and stop flowing into your mind. When you feel this sense of completion and stillness, it is time to close the session.

You may also need to close a session because you are tired from the intense focusing. It is always ok to stop a session! You may disappoint the client, but Heaven understands. If you don't take care of yourself you will lose the joy of being a medium and pretty soon you'll quit doing it completely. So, stop when you feel like you need to or if the session feels done to you.

Thank the client for allowing you to read for them. Then ask them for any feedback they would like to share. Listen and learn.

When you are finished, close your eyes and say a prayer of thanks to yourself for being willing to share your skills and also a prayer of thanks to God for this gift. If you like, you can ask God to bring you more clients and also to help you strengthen your skills even more. Remember, gratitude is the final step and the most important because it increases what you are grateful for!

## Chapter 8

## Difficult Passings

*"I wanted a perfect ending. Now I've learned, the hard way, that some poems don't rhyme, and some stories don't have a clear beginning, middle, and end. Life is about not knowing, having to change, taking the moment and making the best of it, without knowing what's going to happen next."*
*Gilda Radner*

There is one thing I must speak to you about before you attempt to become a medium for other people and that is the topic of difficult passings. No death is easy for those left behind. However, there are two types of passing which can be extremely difficult for family members to deal with- murder and suicide.

Murders unfortunately happen every day in our world. The cruelty we experience as a human race can sometimes seem overwhelming. When that cruelty happens to someone we love it can be unbearable.

Seeking out a medium can give some hope of understanding and peace to the family members. Just knowing that their loved one survives and is doing well can bring deep healing.

I have encountered more souls who have left this Earth in a violent way than I can count. Every single soul, no matter how difficult the passing, brings me an incredible feeling of love and peace to offer their family.

When I detect that a soul has caused their own passing, I will ask them to show me the way they chose to go. I will give simple information to the family member, leaving out any details I feel would be traumatic for them to know about.

I know when a soul has experienced a tragic passing, like murder or suicide, when I feel a tremendous weight on my chest. If the passing was murder, I will feel a pressure on the right side of my throat that makes it difficult to swallow. The left side of my throat indicates suicide, or causing one's own passing- such as a drug overdose or drunk driving.

## Murders

Believe it or not, I have never encountered a soul whose life was taken by another that didn't feel forgiveness for their attacker! As hard as this is for many to hear, those on the other side hold no grudges against those who have taken their lives. The only concern I have ever heard/felt them express is for the family they have left behind.

They will ask me to share their forgiveness with their family members and will even encourage their loved ones to "move on" and forgive the attacker themselves. This can be difficult to repeat as you are looking into the face of a very angry mother who has lost her child to a violent act.

It seems very clear to me after multiple readings that forgiveness is easy for those in heaven. Perhaps it is the ability to understand why their attacker acted the way they did- such as a childhood of abuse and pain, or perhaps it is the awareness of freedom in letting go. Whatever the case, I have never encountered a soul who holds a grudge or feels resentful towards those who did them harm.

There is a deeper wisdom in life of which we don't always understand. That wisdom guides two people together to experience whatever encounter is for the highest good of all- even if it means one of them experiences a violent death. This is a hard thing for our minds to grasp. However, if you look at the changes that one death can create on this earth, you can begin to understand why a soul might agree to leave in this way.

Look at 9/11 as an example. What a tragic experience for our country! I have never seen such an incredible time of heart opening and compassion than I did at that time. We stopped and took notice of what we have. We experienced gratitude for our loved ones and sadness for those who lost their family members to this terrible act. I don't know why it happened, but I do know that not one person lost their life in vain. I noticed and so did you. I cared and so did you. It changed our lives forever.

## Suicide

Suicide is something I hear about almost every time I do readings. It is more common than we talk about. This type of death can bring about so many mixed emotions for the family members. They bounce back and forth between guilt, anger and extreme sadness and confusion.

I have never experienced gratefulness for dying from a soul who took their own life. In fact, it's always the opposite. Suicide ends the physical form but not the suffering. Don't get me wrong. They don't suffer for eternity for the choice they made. It's simply that they realize that their unhappiness was within them and not caused by the world around them. Had they only "stuck it out" they would have seen life improve over time and found great value in their perceived suffering once it shifted.

The soul also experiences the grief of their family members left behind. There is a "buffer" of some sort around the soul, however, which prevents them from being overwhelmed by this grief. I imagine this to be the love of heaven, but am uncertain as to what this is. I can only perceive it around them. The love they feel for those they left behind, who are suffering because of the act of suicide, is the greatest energy of all. They don't seem to desire anything but helping their loved ones to heal.

The soul who took his own life is also surrounded by other loved ones who have passed. They are in no way punished for their action, only loved with deep compassion. Usually these loved ones are there encouraging the soul to let go and forgive themselves for the choice they made.

It's always a wonderful feeling when someone does forgive themselves. It's even better when the family members left behind forgive them too! A great joy and peace is felt in the room. It's almost like you can feel the soul receiving the love of the forgiveness directly. Any heaviness that was felt in the chest at the beginning of the session will lift away and the room feels much lighter.

Every soul that dies be it violent or peaceful, touches the life of every person who knows about it. You could simply read about it in the paper and it touches your life. It has the capacity to make you appreciate each moment of your life, if you allow it to. Let it bring tears to your eyes and open your heart, if you desire. Let this soul, who was a stranger to you before become an awakener to the gift of your life! In doing so, you honor the light that was present within them.

# Chapter 9

## Suggestions from the Author

*"Anybody can do just about anything with himself that he really wants to and makes up his mind to do. We are capable of greater things than we realize."*
**Dr. Norman Vincent Peale**

Practice makes perfect. The more time and effort you give to being a medium the better you will become. There is a balance that must be achieved between doing it enough to learn and doing it too much and losing the joy of it. Don't push yourself ever. Just approach it as something fun to do and you will learn a lot quicker than if you push yourself to practice.

I recommend practicing several times a week for no longer than 30 minutes. You can work your way up to 60 minutes at a time, but give yourself a break after that amount of time.

When I see clients at my office I usually do a 45-50 minute session with a small 5-minute break in between clients. I never exceed 4 sessions per day. I have found that if I do over this amount I stop enjoying the experience.

Doing readings requires a lot of energy and focusing from me. I always know if I am over doing it because I will get a headache and feel very cranky.

You need to be healthy and happy before doing readings. I have had to cancel sessions beforehand because I wasn't feeling healthy. At least 8 hours sleep, lots of water and a nutritious meal are important the day of your readings.

Always eat a light meal before your sessions. Heavy meals, with red meats and carbohydrates will make you sleepy and require a lot of your body's energy for digestion. Try to eat vegetables and fruits with lots and lots of water. Water conducts electricity, so you must be hydrated to pick up those vibrations clearly.

Remember, your joy is most important! If you do not take care of yourself, no one will. Only do a session if you really want to. I have stopped a session right in the middle if I felt a client was unappreciative of the experience. I will refund their money and send them on their way. No money amount is worth being treated poorly.

If you aren't feeling up to a session reschedule it. The client deserves to have you at your best so explain this to them if they question your need to change the appointment. This isn't like a business appointment. Your full self will be required to do a great reading, so make sure you are totally up to it!

Once you develop the skills of a medium, life changes. It's hard for my family, friends, and clients to realize that I am a human being sometimes. When you develop the ability to talk to heaven they may get the misperception that you are a "super human" all of a sudden. They may think you have special access to God or secret information.

Being a medium does not make you better or stronger than anyone! It simply means you have developed a skill of communication. You wouldn't look at someone who could speak another language, such as German, as having all the answers about Germany simply because they could speak the language there. Trusting a medium to have all the answers about the afterlife is unfair to the medium.

Because of this misperception, you may have to be diligent in protecting yourself and your needs. It's hard to say no when someone seems desperate, but you will have to get a thick skin to survive in this field. It's ok to help, as long as it feels good to do so.

As a medium you will change inside and out. You will have a deeper awareness of your own relationship to God. This may give you greater peace and trust in life, but you will not have an easier life or secret answers to life's questions. You will still face challenges and have to figure out your life just like everyone else.

There will not be a halo around your head for all to admire. Once you become a medium, Heaven does not expect you to be good all the time. To be honest with you, I have had more than my share of moments of shame. Being a medium, however, has helped me go easier on myself and forgive my mistakes. I know deep down that I am loved and forgiven.

Because people will seek guidance from you, I do recommend that you work on yourself spiritually. Before I began doing readings for others I did a lot of soul searching. I learned to take responsibility for my life and my own happiness. I explored my inner psyche and got to know my weaknesses and strengths.

There is nothing worse than the blind leading the blind. If you do not know an answer, because you haven't discovered the answer within yourself yet, then say so. Say, "I don't know." You do not need to have all the answers. Don't expect all the answers to be given to you either. There is so much mystery when it comes to life and God. So, never pretend to know it all.

Please remember that what you are doing has value. It is important to honor yourself and the work you will be doing as a medium. After practicing for free on others, you will begin to feel yourself improving enough to charge a fee if you'd like.

In the beginning, you will have hits and misses as you learn the language of heaven. It's not fair to charge someone until you know your service is worth paying for. For me this took about 2 years! I would practice and then take a break of a few weeks and then practice again. It wasn't really my intention in the beginning to make a career out of it. I just loved doing it.

Once you master the skills of being a medium, avoid the assumption that you should offer your services for free just because it deals with God and spirituality. I have never met a minister who didn't get paid. And, for that matter, there is no job on this planet that isn't spiritual in some way because all jobs require us to give of ourselves. So, make sure when you are ready to charge that you support yourself in that decision completely.

When you are about 90% accurate with the information you are receiving during your readings, you are ready to charge a fee. How long it will take you to become this accurate is different for everyone. It's better to not put the pressure on yourself and to trust that you will feel when the time is right.

Be fair with what you charge and you will never have to deal with guilt. There must be an equal energy exchange in any business operation for it to be good for everyone involved.

Ask yourself what you feel you are worth and then trust it. Over time you may increase your price as you get better and the demand for your service grows. This is absolutely ok to do and is a very good business practice.

However, I don't encourage you to take advantage of people's grief and charge huge fees just because you can. I have heard of mediums who basically charge a house payment to get into see them! This is disheartening to hear.

Someone may approach you with a "lack mentality" and tell you they cannot afford the session, in this situation it is up to you to decide what to do. I will usually ask the client what they can afford to pay. I do not believe in free sessions. I believe this only compounds their belief in lack. I remind them that God will provide if they ask and believe. Even if they can barter or exchange their help for services, this is better than nothing.

Once you get better at doing readings, the word will get out about your skill. I have had several occasions where people, having found out what I do, will just walk up to me and start asking me to communicate to the other side for them. I have a personal boundary that I do not allow this. I will tell the person gently, "I don't do readings spontaneously, I like to pray and meditate beforehand. You can schedule an appointment with me if you'd like." Sometimes the person will go ahead and take my information or they will just walk away. You will have to have strong boundaries and self-respect to do this. If you don't, I can guarantee you will lose your interest in being a medium eventually because of the drain on your system.

I also suggest keeping a journal of your sessions. This will help you develop your own lists of symbols and body sensations. I have included all of the ones I have gotten over the years and you may change or add to this if it helps.

If you are simply talking to your own loved ones, always write down the experience and what they choose to communicate to you. The information they communicate may have deeper meaning at a later date. They seem to know where our lives are headed and will often give us helpful words of encouragement.

## Group Readings

Once you practice on individuals and master the skills of a one on one reading, you may decide you want to try group readings. I suggest you begin with no more than 10 people. The only difference in a group reading is that you will first have to feel what person your attention is drawn to the most. From that point on you can proceed as you normally would in a one on one reading.

In a group reading each person will usually get shorter amounts of time with you. You will not get to everyone! Make sure they know this if you are charging a fee.

Before you start, set a time limit for the group reading. I never go over 3 hours and this will include a 20 minute break at the half-way point. During this break time, make sure and go somewhere quiet where you won't be disturbed, drink some water and rest.

When you get comfortable with 10 people go ahead and attempt to increase the number of people. I haven't found any limits on the amount of people you can read! It all boils down to knowing who you are drawn to and focusing all of your attention on that person until it feels complete. Then you can allow your attention to be pulled to someone else in the group. This will go on until you have reached your time limit.

Finally, the most important advice I can give as a medium is- go easy on yourself. Do not expect perfection. Your accuracy will become greater and greater as you learn to listen and receive, but it will never be 100%. If you are hard on yourself you will fail before you ever begin.

I have had students who couldn't take the embarrassment of being even a little bit wrong! If you are afraid of being wrong and won't let yourself speak up, then this isn't really for you.

A little fear of failure is normal, but your desire to succeed must be greater. This is why practicing on others for free at first can help to remove the pressure of being perfect. Tell the client you may be wrong about some things since you are just beginning, but that you will try your best. You may be surprised how helpful they will seem and how relaxed it helps you to be.

When I first began to give readings I would get so nervous that I would shake and my palms would get sweaty. I had tremendous butterflies in my stomach and most of the time would want to quit before I even started. The bigger the group I was reading the greater the shakiness.

One day I decided to ask why this was happening. The answer I got from within was, "Your vibration is being raised to make it easier for you to connect. This can cause shakiness and a feeling of anxiety. It will pass with time." My inner guidance was correct. Now, when I do readings I am calm and peaceful the entire time.

This gift of being a medium is given freely to all who ask and believe. So, go ahead and ask! If it brings you joy to think about doing it, then you are listening to your heart in the pursuit of this skill. There is no other reason to even attempt it. Joy is our reason for living.

If we listen to our hearts and follow our bliss, we will find ourselves in acts of true service. True service grows out of joy. So, you aren't really serving if you aren't enjoying what you are doing. Always listen to your heart and do only what feels joyful to you. Take your time and never push yourself past feeling good.

**Namaste ~ *Rev. Martina Schmidt***

# Appendix A

## Crossing Over Symbols

**Pink Rose** - New Baby Girl in family

**Blue Rose** - New Baby Boy

**White Cross** - Recent Baptism/ Confirmation in the family

**Red Roses** -Wedding Anniversary

**Wedding Bells**- Recent or Upcoming Wedding

**Balloons/ Wrapped Present**- Acknowledging a recent Birthday usually within a 2-week time frame of the session-before or after

**A heart**- Indicates a love connection/relationship with the client

**Egg**- New beginning for the client- like new home or job

**American Flag**- Someone who was in the armed services

**Country Flag**- Such as France, Germany, means they were from this country

**Book**- Indicates someone is a writer/author

**Bible**-Indicates minister/priest in family

**Fire**- Indicates passing in a fire

**Water**- Indicates drowning

**Rainbow**- Indicates a young child passed

**Animals**- Cats, dogs, horses, rabbits may indicate pets that have crossed; not always indicative of the breed just the animal

**Rings or Necklaces** may be pointed at in your mind to indicate a connection to the person- such as they are wearing a piece of jewelry given to them by the person you are speaking to on the other side. They may also point at a wedding ring to indicate they are the spouse of the client.

**Numbers** relate to month or date of significance- such as birthday or death date for example 7 could be July or the 7th of a month

# Write your own symbols here:

## Appendix B

## Body Sensations That Indicate Means of Passing

1.  Right Armpit pain in lymph area- Cancer or Immune System Disease like HIV/AIDS

2.  Back of Heart- Heart Attack

3.  Chest Heavy- Lung Disease, Respiratory Problems

4.  Chest feels like someone is sitting on you- Accident where person was crushed or impacted something with the body. This is much stronger than the chest heavy sensations above. It will feel hard to talk because it is so heavy.

5.  Trachea pressure on right side of throat- murdered or life taken by another's carelessness

6.  Left side of Throat squeezed- suicide or caused own passing through drug use or careless behavior

7.  Sensation in Breast Area- Breast Cancer

8.  Uterus/ lower abdomen pain- usually lost pregnancy or female reproductive disease

9.  Kidneys- kidney failure

10. Right Upper abdomen pressure- liver problems or pancreas

11. Alcohol on Breath- alcoholic- you will usually feel pressure on the right side of abdomen in liver area with this

12. Smoke in mouth or smell of smoke in air- smoker

13. Bitter taste in mouth like aspirin- Heavily medicated when died

14. Stomach pressure- if deep in body this indicates an aneurysm, if lighter sensation then it is usually stomach cancer (however you will also feel the arm pit pain on the right side to indicate Cancer)

15. You may get heaviness in your legs which indicate a wheelchair was needed or that there was paralysis

16. If you feel pressure in your head then it could be several things:

    - A stroke in which case I also feel tightness in my throat at the same time I feel pressure in my head
    - A mental illness such as depression
    - Unconsciousness when they passed
    - Or a head injury

**List your own sensations here:**

# Appendix C

## Body Placement for
## Determining Relationship to Client

(The chart represents the client as you are facing them)
You will feel drawn to an area that will indicate if the soul
communicating with you is male/female and older (above),
same generation (beside) or younger (below) the client.

If they are not related to the client but simply a friend they
will draw your attention in front of the client and out to the
side, as if they were looking at the client or they will feel
"detached" from the client's body.

This takes some practice to fine tune! Pay attention to any
quick, small bursts of light you see in your peripheral vision.
This will happen sometimes when a soul is trying to get your
attention, like a "look here" signal.

Pets will sometimes lay there head on your foot to get your
attention. So, pay attention to a sudden feeling of pressure on
the top of your feet or lap area.

Males                           Females

Uncles (*)                      (*) Aunts

Husband, Father or (*X)         (*⁎) Mother, Grandmothers, Wife
Grandfathers                        (Above Shoulders)
(Above Shoulders)
Male Siblings, Cousins (*)      (*) Female Siblings, Cousins
                                     (shoulder level)

Male Children *                      * Female
(son, nephews)                         Children
grandchildren                          (daughter, niece)
                                       grandchildren

                *
Male Pets/                           * Female Animals/Pets
Animals

                *                    *

# *Notes*

# <u>*Notes*</u>

# Other Items by Rev. Martina Schmidt

Items may be purchased by ordering online
***www.martinaschmidt.com***

1. **Connecting with Heaven Guided Meditation Audio CD**
   This audio cd gives you the guided meditation listed in this book. It also contains an explanation of heaven and mediumship.

   Price $14.95

2. **Using the Pendulum for Greater Awareness**
   This is a flip chart book on the different chakras in which you can use a pendulum to determine where your inner growth needs to be focused.

   Price $11.95

3. **Meditations for Wellness Audio CD**
   This audio cd contains 3 different guided meditations, approx. 20 mins. in length. These meditations are designed to guide you to greater awareness of your body, mind and spirit connection.

   Price $14.95

CPSIA information can be obtained at www.ICGtesting.com
Printed in the USA
LVOW12s2007160315

430778LV00001B/166/P